$21.24

10/17

45

ROCK-OLOGY
The Hard Facts
About Rocks

How Do People Use Rocks?

by Ellen Lawrence

Consultants:

Shawn W. Wallace
Department of Earth and Planetary Sciences
American Museum of Natural History, New York, New York

Kimberly Brenneman, PhD
National Institute for Early Education Research, Rutgers University
New Brunswick, New Jersey

BEARPORT
PUBLISHING

New York, New York

Credits

Cover, © Robert Crum/Shutterstock; 2–3, © WitR/Shutterstock; 4–5, © Songquan Deng/Shutterstock; 5TL, © Siim Sepp/ Shutterstock; 5TR, © Angela Waye/Shutterstock; 6T, © Gianni Dagli Orti/Alamy; 6B, © Public Domain; 7, © Anthony Page; 7R, © Public Domain; 8, © Reinhard Dirscheri/Alamy; 9, © WitR/Shutterstock; 10T, © Andrew F. Kazmierski/Shutterstock; 10BL, © Chris Pole/Thinkstock; 10BR, © mujdatuzel/Istockphoto; 11, © Alexandra Lande/Shutterstock; 12, © Robynrg/ Shutterstock; 13, © Sarah Jessup/Shutterstock; 13R, © Alison Hancock/Shutterstock; 14, © Cultura Limited/Superstock; 15, © Kathryn Allen Hurni/Corbis; 15T, © CDPiC/Shutterstock; 16T, © Siim Sepp/Shutterstock; 16CL, © Chris Parypa Photography/Shutterstock; 16CR, © Sukharevskyy Dmytro (nevodka)/Shutterstock; 16B, © Vladimir Wrangel/Shutterstock; 17T, © Fokin Oleg/Shutterstock; 17, © Snap2Art/Shutterstock; 18TL, © Phil Degginger/Jack Clark Collection/Alamy; 18TR, © Erhan Dayi/Shutterstock; 18CL, © StrangerThanKindness/Wikipedia Creative Commons; 18CR, © Kulish Viktoriia/Shutterstock; 18BL, © farbled/Shutterstock; 18BR, © creativepro/Shutterstock; 19L, © Imfoto/Shutterstock; 19R, © teena137/Shutterstock; 20T, © Marcio Jose Bastos Silva/Shutterstock; 20B, © Louie Psihoyos/Corbis; 21, © Layne Kennedy/Corbis; 22, © Bogdan Ionescu/Shutterstock, © studioVin/Shutterstock, © OlegSam/Shutterstock, © My name is boy/Shutterstock, © Tom Grundy/ Shutterstock, © Sergiy Kuzmin/Shutterstock, © Jiri Vaclavek/Shutterstock, and © Vladimir Wrangel/Shutterstock; 23TL, © Public Domain; 23TC, © Alison Hancock/Shutterstock; 23TR, © StrangerThanKindness/Wikipedia Creative Commons; 23BL, © Jaroslav Moravcik/Shutterstock; 23BC, © Stefano Cavoretto/Shutterstock; 23BR, © Ververidis Vasilis/Shutterstock.

Publisher: Kenn Goin
Editorial Director: Adam Siegel
Creative Director: Spencer Brinker
Project Editor: Natalie Lunis
Photo Researcher: Ruby Tuesday Books Ltd

Library of Congress Cataloging-in-Publication Data

Lawrence, Ellen, 1967–
 How do people use rocks? / by Ellen Lawrence.
   pages cm. — (Rock-ology)
 Audience: Age 5-8.
 Includes bibliographical references and index.
 ISBN 978-1-62724-303-2 (library binding) — ISBN 1-62724-303-8 (library binding)
 1. Rocks—Juvenile literature. 2. Minerals—Juvenile literature. 3. Industrial minerals—Juvenile literature. I.
Title.
 QE432.2.L39 2015
 553—dc23

                    2014012053

For more information, write to Bearport Publishing Company, Inc., 45 West 21st Street, Suite 3B,
New York, New York 10010. Printed in the United States of America.

10 9 8 7 6 5 4 3 2 1

Contents

Rocks in Our World

Every day, you see and use rock—sometimes without knowing it.

Houses, schools, and other buildings are often made out of rock.

Rocks are needed to make cars and computers.

Even the grayish-black part of a pencil comes from rock.

In fact, people have been using rock in hundreds of different ways for millions of years!

Rocks are made up of solid substances called **minerals**. A rock can be made up of just one mineral or several different minerals. The part of a pencil that writes is made from a mineral called graphite.

rock containing graphite

graphite in a pencil

The towers of the Brooklyn Bridge in New York City are made out of rock.

Stone Age Rocks

Ancient Stone Age people made weapons for hunting animals from rock.

They carved pointed tips for spears from a kind of rock called flint.

They also made sharp cutting tools called hand axes for cutting up meat.

Stone Age people even made their homes in rocky caves.

They had no paper for painting pictures, so they painted on the walls of caves.

flint spear tip

Stone Age hand ax

The Stone Age began about three million years ago. It ended about 6,000 years ago. This time in history is called the Stone Age because people made tools from stone, or rock.

Stone Age caves in
Creswell Crags, England

cave entrance

Stone Age people created pictures
of animals and people using paint
made from rocks. How do you
think they made their paint?

(The answer is on page 24.)

Rock Pyramids

Since ancient times, people have used rock to make amazing buildings.

About 4,500 years ago, people in Egypt built huge rock pyramids.

They buried their kings and queens inside them.

The Great Pyramid of Giza is the largest.

It is made from more than two million giant blocks of limestone and granite rock.

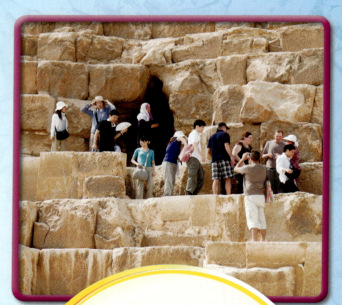

Many of the blocks of rock used to build the Great Pyramid weigh more than an elephant. The pyramid builders had no cranes or trucks. No one knows for sure how they moved and lifted the huge pieces of rock.

When it was built, the Great Pyramid was 481 feet (147 m) tall. Today it is a little shorter because rocks on the top have crumbled away or been stolen.

How Tall Is the Great Pyramid?

height (in feet)

600
500
400
300
200
100
0

Statue of Liberty
305 feet (93 m)

The Great Pyramid
481 feet (147 m)

Washington Monument
555 feet (169 m)

the Great Pyramid

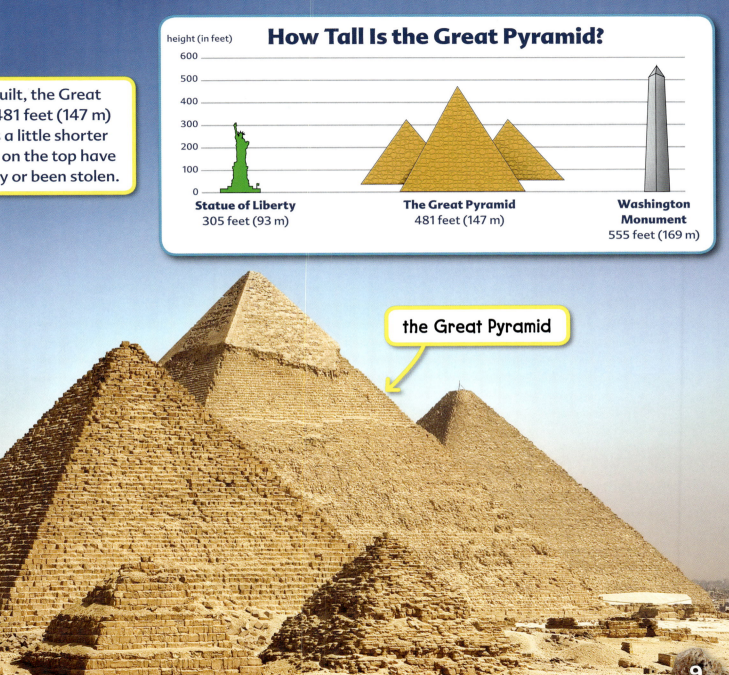

Rock for Statues

People have been using rock to make statues for thousands of years.

Many famous statues are made from a kind of rock called marble.

To make a statue, a sculptor starts with a large chunk of marble.

Then the sculptor chips away pieces of the rock using a hammer and chisel.

When the shape is finished, the sculptor rubs the marble with sandpaper to make it smooth.

a marble lion outside the New York Public Library

hammer

chisel

sculptor

Taj Mahal

The Taj Mahal is a building in India. It was built by an emperor as a burial place for his wife. The building is made from marble that is covered with beautiful carvings.

Building with Rock Today

Rock isn't found just in statues and buildings from long ago.

Today, people live in homes built from granite, sandstone, and other kinds of rock.

Rock is also crushed and mixed with water and other materials to make **concrete**.

The concrete is then used to build skyscrapers and other buildings.

Concrete is also used to make roads, sidewalks, and skateboard parks.

a house built from rock

Where do you think people get the rocks to construct buildings?

concrete ramp

When concrete is first made, it is a thick liquid. The wet mixture is poured into the place where it is needed. After a short time, the mixture dries and hardens.

Rock from Quarries

Rock, such as granite, is dug up at a huge, deep hole called a **quarry**.

Workers at the quarry begin by setting off an explosion.

The explosion breaks off a house-sized chunk of rock.

Then machines cut the chunk of rock into smaller blocks—each one the size of a car.

Finally, a crane lifts the blocks from the quarry.

Trucks deliver the rock to factories, where it is cut into smaller blocks for building.

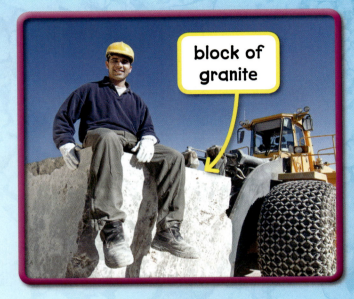

block of granite

At some quarries, rock is dug from the ground and crushed into tiny pieces. This crushed rock is used for making concrete.

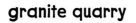
granite quarry

Look at this crushed rock. It can be used to make concrete and also used in another way. What do you think the other way could be?

(The answer is on page 24.)

house-sized chunk of rock

Metals from Rock

Rocks are very useful because of the minerals they contain.

For example, metals, such as aluminum and iron, are really minerals that are found in rocks.

Aluminum can come from a kind of rock called bauxite (BAWK-site).

This metal is used for making planes, frying pans, foil, and soda cans.

Iron can come from sandstone rock.

It is used to make steel, which is needed for making cars and other vehicles.

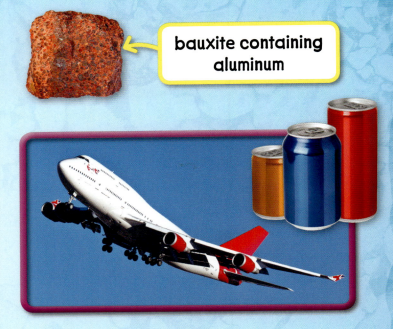

bauxite containing aluminum

Copper and nickel are also minerals that come from rocks. These metals are used to make coins such as pennies and nickels.

car made with steel

sandstone containing iron

Jewelry from Rocks

Sometimes, minerals in rocks form in shapes called **crystals**.

Some crystals are very beautiful and colorful.

These crystals are removed from rocks, cut, and polished.

Then the crystals are known as gemstones and are used to make jewelry.

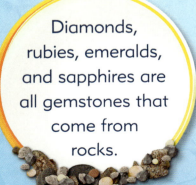

Diamonds, rubies, emeralds, and sapphires are all gemstones that come from rocks.

diamond crystal in rock

ruby crystal in rock

emerald crystal in rock

sapphire
crystal

sapphire
gemstone

Learning from Rocks

There's one very surprising way in which rocks are useful.

Sometimes people find **fossils** in them.

Fossils are the rocky remains of animals and plants that lived millions of years ago.

Without rocks, people wouldn't know that dinosaurs existed.

That means that Earth's rocks aren't just useful for making things.

We can also learn from them!

fish fossil

People have found dinosaur footprints in rock.

rock

fossil of a *Tyrannosaurus rex* skull

21

Science Lab

Rocks-and-Minerals Treasure Hunt

Go on a rocks-and-minerals treasure hunt to see how many of the things on the list below you can find. You can look in your home, in a backyard, at the park, or even at the beach. Some of the items on the list are rocks or are made from rocks. Others are made from minerals found in rocks. Collect as many objects as possible. Then do a show-and-tell for your family, friends, or teacher.

Treasure Hunt List

gravel

a rock that can be used as a tool
Try to find a piece of rock that could be used as a tool—just like Stone Age people did. What kinds of jobs can your stone tool do?

a rock that contains crystals
Try using a magnifying glass to look for sparkly crystals in rocks.

sand
Sand is made of tiny pieces of rock. Sand on a beach is often made by waves crashing against rocky cliffs, causing pieces of rock to break off.

a pencil with graphite inside

a paper clip
Paper clips are made from steel, which contains iron.

aluminum foil

a dime

ancient (AYN-shuhnt) very old; from long-ago times

concrete (KON-kreet) a hard material used in construction; it is made by mixing crushed rock, sand, water, and cement, which is rock that has been crushed into a powder

crystals (KRISS-tuhlz) solid minerals that have formed in shapes that have straight edges and smooth sides

fossils (FOSS-uhlz) what is left of animals or plants that lived long ago

minerals (MIN-ur-uhlz) the solid substances that make up rocks

quarry (KWOR-ee) a place in the ground or along the side of a hill where rock is cut

Index

Read More

Colich, Abby. *Metal (Exploring Materials)*. North Mankato, MN: Heinemann (2014).

Katz Cooper, Sharon. *Using Rocks (Exploring Earth's Resources)*. North Mankato, MN: Heinemann (2007).

Roza, Greg. *Exploring Rocks and Minerals (Exploring Earth and Space)*. New York: Rosen (2013).

Learn More Online

To learn more about how people use rocks, visit **www.bearportpublishing.com/Rock-ology**

About the Author

Ellen Lawrence lives in the United Kingdom. Her favorite books to write are those about nature and animals. In fact, the first book Ellen bought for herself, when she was six years old, was the story of a gorilla named Patty Cake that was born in New York's Central Park Zoo.

Answers

Page 7: The minerals that make up rocks are sometimes bright colors. For example, ocher (OH-kur) is a mineral that comes in many colors, including red. Stone Age people crushed up rocks to get the minerals. Then they mixed the crushed minerals with water to make paint.

Page 15: Crushed rock is known as gravel. It is used as a covering for paths and driveways.